SEABIRDS

SEABIRDS

Mark J. Rauzon

A First Book

FRANKLIN WATTS   *A Division of Grolier Publishing*
New York • London • Hong Kong • Sydney • Danbury, Connecticut

To Craig S. Harrison

Frontispiece: A flock of white pelicans look for food.
Photo credits ©: Academy of Natural Sciences: pp. 28, 33 (both photos Mark J. Rauzon);
Comstock: p. 11 (Phyllis Greenberg); Mark J. Rauzon: pp. 2, 13, 31, 34, 40;
Photo Researchers : pp. 8 (Francois Gohier), 18 (George Holton), 25 (Rod Planck),
45 (Tim Davis), 47 (Nigel Dennis), 48 (Jany Sauvanet), 50 (Rod Planck); Superstock, Inc.:
pp. 14, 17; Visuals Unlimited: cover (Nada Pecnik), pp. 20, 36 (both photos Joe
McDonald), 23 (David L. Pearson), 26 (Barbara Gerlach), 39, 52, 58 (all photos Kjell B.
Sandved), 42 (Arthur Morris), 54 (John Gerlach), 57 (John Lough).

Library of Congress Cataloging-in-Publication Data

Rauzon, Mark J.
Seabirds / Mark J. Rauzon.
p. cm. — (A First book)
Includes bibliographical references and index.
Summary: Describes different kinds of sea birds, including gulls,
terns, albatrosses, cormorants, pelicans, and penguins.
ISBN 0-531-20246-1 (lib.bdg.) 1SBN 0-531-15817-9 (pbk.)
1. Sea birds—Juvenile literature. [1. Sea birds. 2. Birds.]
I. Title. II. Series.
QL676.2.R36 1996
598.29'24—dc20   96-7185 CIP AC
© 1996 by Mark J. Rauzon
All rights reserved. Published simultaneously in Canada
Printed in the United States of America
1 2 3 4 5 6 7 8 9 10 R 05 04 03 02 01 00 99 98 97 96

CONTENTS

SEABIRDS

Thousands of northern gannets flock to sea cliffs to nest.

CHAPTER ONE

WHERE THE WIND MEETS THE WAVES

The seabird's world is the air and the ocean, from the breaking surf to the open sea. Beachcombers and blue-water sailors can see over 320 kinds, or species, of seabirds in seventeen families in all the oceans of the world. Whether it's gulls soaring on brisk breezes, pelicans plunging into the surf, or penguins swimming through the icy ocean, seabirds are the most visible of all the ocean animals. The major seabird groups include penguins; puffins and other auks; pelicans, cormorants, and boobies; albatrosses, shearwaters, and petrels; and gulls and terns.

In order to survive where the wind meets the waves, seabirds have become expert fliers and divers. Some seabirds can soar on the ocean winds for miles without flapping. When they spot food, they quickly dive down to pluck prey from the sea. With stout bills, seabirds grab and tear apart fish, crabs, and other animals. Seabirds swim expertly in the ocean with their webbed feet, and some fly underwater with their wings. With sharp eyes usually shaded to block the sun's glare off the water, they can find food in the roughest seas.

Seabirds need all these skills plus a little luck to find and catch food in the vast ocean. The ocean produces an abundance of food, but the supply ebbs and flows. The amount of food available in the ocean at any one time depends on sunlight, water currents, dissolved nutrients, and sea temperature.

Sunlight causes algae and other tiny plants called plankton to grow in the seawater. These tiny plants grow best where underwater currents bring dissolved nutrients from the ocean floor to the sunny surface. Nutrients dissolved in seawater fertilize the plankton, which can turn the sea green and brown.

Cold water can hold more oxygen than warm water. Since oxygen is necessary for life, more animals can live in cold water than in warm water. The warm waters of the tropical oceans are sometimes without any sign of life for many square miles. With little plankton to color them, the tropics have clear blue waters.

A brown pelican dives for food.

The icy Arctic and Antarctic waters, which are cloudy and greenish from plankton, teem with sea life.

Patches of plankton attract schools of krill, a type of red shrimp. They in turn feed small fish. Larger fish and squid come to eat the smaller ones and attract even bigger fish. The big fish chase the small ones to the sea surface, where they cannot escape. Here, many species of seabirds are watching and waiting. When seabirds see another seabird diving into the schools of fish, they fly in from far away to catch their fill.

Seabirds have evolved ways to get food without competing with each other. Each species has its own manner of fishing. The main fishing techniques used are surface seizing, plunge diving, and pursuit diving.

Some birds, like gulls, seize prey from the surface with their stout beaks. Gulls sit on the water and thrust their heads underwater to grab for food. Terns may dip beneath the surface to catch small fish. Black skimmers fly just above the water with their lower bill slicing the surface. When the lower bill touches a fish, the upper bill snaps shut instantly to seize the prey.

Like some other seabirds, pelicans are plunge divers. From the air, pelicans spy fish swimming deep in the water, fold their wings, and drop from the sky like an arrow. Plunging underwater, they open their throat pouches, surround the fish, and snap the upper beak shut. Brown pelicans can dive from 60 feet (18 m) in the air. They smack the water with great force, but air bags under their neck skins absorb the shock of hitting the water's hard surface. Tropicbirds and boobies are the most spectacular plunge divers, seizing their prey underwater with a quick stab of their beaks.

Black skimmers seize food from the water surface.

Other seabirds duck underwater and pursue fish. Cormorants sink like submarines and chase fish by kicking with their powerful legs while their snakelike necks reach out to nab fleeing fish. Puffins literally fly underwater with their wings. Their feet act as rudders to steer as they speed through the water. No seabird, however, can swim underwater like the penguin.

Emperor penguins huddle with chicks on an Antarctic ice pack.

THE PENGUINS

Penguins have developed flipperlike wings to increase their speed underwater. With flippers and torpedo-shaped bodies, penguins swim faster than most fish. The closest they come to flying is when they leap out of the water like porpoises to breathe.

Penguins are also too heavy to fly because they are wrapped in dense, furlike feathers and thick blubber. The penguin's insulation is like a wet suit to protect it from cold water, rough waves, sharp rocks, and ice. Penguins are adapted to life in the cold waters of the Southern Hemisphere and do not live in the North.

Standing over 3 feet (91 cm) tall and weighing an average of 66 pounds (30 kg), emperor penguins are the heaviest seabirds. They also breed in the most extreme weather conditions on earth.

In the complete darkness of the Antarctic winter, the male cradles a single egg on his feet. He huddles together with other males to reduce the windchill from blizzard conditions. For about sixty days, he stands on the pack ice, guarding the egg while the female is feeding at sea. She returns to the nest by tobogganing on her stomach, for they often nest many miles from the sea. Although he is very reluctant to leave the chick with the female, the male penguin has lost almost half of his weight and must feed himself or risk starving to death. If he starves, the chick will also die, since both parents must feed the chick until it is fully grown. Chicks grow so slowly that emperor penguins can breed only every other year.

The smaller Adélie penguins nest on stony plateaus, often in immense colonies around Antarctic research stations. Adélies look as if they are dressed in black and white tuxedos. They lay two eggs and if food is abundant, they can raise both chicks. While feeding, the penguins may themselves become food for predators like leopard seals and killer whales.

Some penguin species live away from icy areas but near cold waters. Huge colonies of Magellanic penguins

An Adélie penguin chick begs for food.

Yellow-eyed penguins are the rarest penguins in the world.

live at the tip of South America. Over one million penguins leave the cold water to nest in a colony on the desert coast of Argentina. With much loud braying and fighting, these penguins dig burrows in the dry earth and lay a pair of eggs. For about six months, this ruckus continues until the adults and young return to the sea. It must be a shock the first time a young penguin plunges into the cold ocean.

Just over 1 foot (30 cm) high, little blue penguins are the smallest penguins. They are also the most commonly seen group of penguins. Large numbers come ashore to nest along the coasts of southern Australia and New Zealand. Sitting on their nests under boathouses or docks, little blue penguins hee-haw like mules. They lay two eggs, which they guard for several months. To feed the growing youngsters, parents must swim out to sea daily to gather shrimp. They waddle up the beach at night in a group for protection.

The rarest penguins of all are the yellow-eyed penguins. Their world population numbers only several thousand. They can be seen on the southern island of New Zealand, where they come ashore to nest in dense vegetation around sheep farms. It is here that farm dogs and cats catch and kill these rare penguins.

The black-and-white razorbill is the largest kind of auk.

THE PUFFINS AND OTHER AUKS

Puffins are the best-known members of the auk family. Other family members include murres, murrelets, auklets, and guillemots. Auks are the northern counterparts of the penguins of the South. Auks and penguins look similar because they have adapted to similar environmental conditions: icy-cold water.

Like penguins, puffins and their kin fly underwater by flapping their wings. Unlike penguins, these black-and-white birds can also fly in the air. They are plump birds with short wings and must flap constantly to stay airborne. They nest on tall sea cliffs and must dive off and flap madly to get up enough speed to fly.

The auk most similar to the penguin, the great auk, has disappeared from the face of the earth. Since the great auks were flightless, they nested on low, flat islands in the North Atlantic Ocean and became easy targets for Vikings, fishermen, and sailors looking for food and fish bait. Sadly, the last birds were killed in 1844 by greedy collectors who wanted specimens for their museums before the great auks completely disappeared. The great auk was one of the first North American birds to become extinct. Another seabird, the Labrador duck, soon followed the auk into extinction.

Great auks resembled their close relatives, the common murres. Since murres can fly, they nest on narrow ledges of tall sea cliffs, safe from predators. Huddled together, they look like bowling pins. Without building a nest, they lay one egg on a narrow ledge. The greenish egg is pointed on one end. If the egg rolls, it spins in a tight circle so it won't fall off the cliff.

The ledge, however, is no place to raise an energetic young bird. For that reason, when the chick is still small, the male parent coaxes it to jump off the cliff into the sea. The male joins it and teaches the young one to fish.

Murrelets are small murres. The marbled murrelet is unique among seabirds. While many seabird species

Common murres lay greenish eggs on the narrow ledges of Newfoundland sea cliffs.

nest in the ground among the roots of trees, the marbled murrelet nests in the tops of old trees, on the wide, moss-covered branches.

The marbled murrelet is threatened with extinction through loss of its habitat. In northern California, Oregon, Washington, and Alaska, these seabirds nest in big trees that are being cut down for lumber. It is impossible to know exact population counts since they fly into their treetop nests only at night. They also face threats at sea, where many drown in gill nets set for fish. If the marbled murrelet population continues its decline, it could join its famous extinct relative, the great auk.

Auklets are the smallest members of the auk family. Flocks of auklets number in the millions on predator-free islands. The Aleutian Islands of western Alaska is home to many auklets.

The crested, least, parakeet, whiskered, and Cassin's auklets nest in rock crevices and burrows in the earth. In the summer, these auklets show off for their mates with their plumes and colorful beaks. In the winter, they shed their plumes and orange beaks and develop a dull-brown beak.

The crested auklet is an unusual seabird because it smells sweet. The orange beak of the crested auklet not

The orange beaks of crested auklets smell like tangerines.

only looks like but smells like tangerines. The least auklet, which lives in some of the roughest seas and stormiest weather on earth, weighs only a few ounces. Surprisingly, the rhinoceros auklet, which has a horn on its bill, is not an auklet at all. Although its horn and whiskers make the rhinoceros auklet look like the largest auklet, its closest relative is actually the puffin.

Puffins are plump seabirds that nest in rocky crevices and deep burrows that they dig in grassy slopes above the sea. With yellow-feathered tassels flipping like corn silk in the wind over their eyes, tufted puffins look like the clowns of the seabird world. The horned puffin has a fleshy spike above its eye and is found in the North Pacific Ocean. The common puffin resides in the North Atlantic Ocean. Because of their big colorful beaks, puffins are sometimes called sea parrots. But beware— a puffin can crush a person's finger with its beak.

The Atlantic puffin can catch and hold fish easily with its sharp bill.

During nesting season, male frigatebirds inflate red pouches under their beaks.

PELICANS, TROPICBIRDS, AND FRIGATEBIRDS

Pelicans, cormorants, boobies and gannets, tropicbirds, and frigatebirds are all related. They all have colorful faces and throat pouches. They also all have totipalmate feet, which means that all four toes are connected by webbing. These seabirds are awkward on land but swim skillfully both on and under the water.

Everyone knows a pelican's bill "holds more than its belly can." When fully expanded, the pelican's bill can hold 2 gallons (7.6 l) of water. Relatives of the pelican have pouches too. The male frigatebird inflates the red skin under his beak and rattles his beak on it to attract a female's attention.

Cormorants have colorful throats and faces. Pelagic cormorants have scarlet skin, and Brandt's cormorants have electric-blue skin during the breeding season. Double-crested cormorants have yellow throats and faces. In the summer heat, they flutter their throats to keep cool, much the way dogs pant. Their large throats are also a feeding basin for the young. Parents regurgitate fish—bringing it up from the crop, or stomach—into the throat, and the chicks feed.

Cormorants are submarine divers. Because these birds lack oil glands, their feathers become quickly soaked and they easily sink. Instead of paddling with their wings underwater like penguins, cormorants paddle with their webbed feet. After diving, they spread their waterlogged wings to dry, for they cannot fly with wet feathers. Other seabirds, with waterproof feathers, stay high and dry. To stay waterproof, they squeeze oil from the gland located at the base of their tail with their beaks and preen it into their feathers.

Cormorants use their feet to keep their eggs and chicks warm. The featherless chicks are cradled on top of the parents' warm feet until they grow their own white down. As the chicks grow bigger, brown feathers replace the down. Double-crested cormorants nest in groups or colonies built on stony cliffs, islands, or trees. In San Francisco Bay, they nest under bridges, out of the sight of passing cars and trucks.

Double-crested cormorant chicks feed from their parent's throat.

Boobies are tropical seabirds. These birds evolved on islands with few animals to fear. They are called boobies because they are so tame and easy to approach; sailors needed only to hit them on the head to get a meal. Their name comes from the Spanish word *bobo*, which means stupid.

The blue-footed booby and the red-footed booby use their colorful feet during breeding displays. The blue-footed booby parades in front of the female, making sure she sees his feet. Flashing his blood-red feet, the red-footed booby lands on the female's back and presents her with a stick before mating.

Boobies have evolved in such a way that all the species share the limited food of the warm tropical seas. Brown boobies make shallow dives into shallow nearshore waters. Red-footed boobies fly far out at sea and catch small flying fish. Masked boobies—the largest boobies—take big flying fish from the ocean waters.

Gannets are closely related to boobies. Gannets, however, are found in cold water like that in northeastern Canada, southern Africa, Australia, and New Zealand. Like boobies and pelicans, these white birds plunge headfirst into the ocean. When a school of fish

A red-footed booby brings a stick to his mate.

Red-tailed tropicbirds can fly backward.

is sighted, the birds close their wings and plummet toward their target.

Onshore, gannets nest in colonies, where they cement their seaweed and feather nests together with bird waste matter, or guano. Immature birds attain the snow-white adult plumage in three to four years and may breed after six years.

During the old sailing days when frigates were the fastest ships, pirates often used them to make a speedy getaway. The sailors saw the same thing in the world of seabirds. They named the fastest seabirds great frigate-birds or man o' war birds because they could steal food from and fly faster than other birds.

Frigatebirds chase boobies and terns to rob them of their daily catch. They are able to fly so fast because they weigh so little. Frigatebirds have hollow wing bones fitted with internal struts, like airplane wings, which give them great flying capabilities.

Tropicbirds are also excellent fliers. The white-tailed tropicbirds race on trade winds in the mountains of Hawaii and plunge into the clear Pacific Ocean from high above. The red-tailed tropicbird can even fly back-wards. Wheeling around each other during courtship displays, their long, thin tail feathers flutter as they fly during the hottest part of the day.

Albatrosses have special nostrils that excrete salt water.

THE
TUBENOSES

All seabirds can drink salt water. Because too much salt can kill, seabirds get rid of salt through special glands located in their heads. The glands concentrate the salt water and excrete it through their beaks. Some seabirds have special tubes on their beaks. Drops of salty water roll out through the tubes on their upper bills and drip from the tip of their beaks. Called tubenoses, these birds include albatrosses, storm petrels, and shearwaters.

Tubenoses feed their chicks a form of stomach oil. This smelly, orange, gooey liquid is made from digested squid. When threatened with danger, some species of petrels will spit this oil at intruders.

The tubenose group includes both the largest and smallest flying seabirds. Spanning 5.5 inches (14 cm), the least storm petrels are the smallest seabirds. With an 11-foot (3-m) wingspan, wandering albatrosses are the largest of all flying birds.

The long, narrow wings of the wandering albatross are well suited for gliding on the wild winds common out on the Antarctic Ocean. These great albatrosses fly around the world where the ocean winds sweep across thousands of miles. They use the energy of the wind to rise up in the air and then they coast downward. By repeating this flight style, called dynamic soaring, over and over again, they save their energy. These ocean wanderers can fly hundreds of miles each day hunting for food without flapping their wings.

The huge but tame albatrosses nest in colonies on grassy cliffs or on islands. They usually return to where they were hatched to raise one chick every other year. From four to nine years pass before the chicks return to breed, and they may spend years at sea without ever touching land. Even during storms, albatrosses ride the wind. Indeed, during a storm, it is safer to be airborne than on the rough water.

Albatrosses have impressive navigation skills and can return to their nesting islands from practically anywhere. In one experiment, scientists captured several Laysan albatrosses and transported them far away from their Hawaiian

A pair of albatrosses ride the wind.

Fork-tailed storm petrels walk on water.

homes. One albatross was taken 3,200 miles (5,150 km) from home and it returned to its nest in just twelve days!

No bigger than a starling, the fork-tailed storm petrel is able to survive the same weather and winds as the giant albatrosses. The small bird covers thousands of miles each year. When it descends to the sea surface to catch food, the storm petrel seems to "walk on water" like its namesake, Saint Peter. With their wings held aloft by wind, they grace the oceans with their mastery of flight, picking small crustaceans from the sea surface.

Another group of tubenoses, the shearwaters, streak over the waves, slicing the water with their wing tips. Some migrate more than 20,000 miles (32,200 km) each year from their nesting grounds in Australia to Alaskan waters. The remarkable migration of the short-tailed shearwater spans virtually the entire Pacific Ocean. They nest in burrows dug into islets off the coast of Australia. After nesting, they travel north in a clockwise direction, following the east coast of Asia to reach the waters of Alaska by the summer. Millions of short-tailed shearwaters congregate here to feast on the abundant krill. Winter weather drives the birds down the west coast of North America. Around California, the shearwaters angle southwest and return to their breeding grounds in time to nest again.

This herring gull chick lives on Long Island, New York.

GULLS AND TERNS

Almost everyone has seen a gull. Because they benefit from living close to humans, gulls have become abundant. They forage for food in harbors and dumps. Some gulls will eat almost anything. Herring gulls in New York dumps eat French fries and hot dogs, while great black-backed gulls in Maine eat a healthier diet of both live and dead fish, small mammals, and birds. From their island nests, they can steal the eggs and chicks of any bird, including other gulls.

Some gulls may live for thirty years if they can find food in the ever changing ocean environment. Ivory gulls are all-white marine gulls of the northern seas. They nest on sea cliffs and winter far out on the icy sea, scavenging the ice pack for food. Silver gulls are common in Australia and New Zealand, where they frequent harbors and bays looking for fish and garbage. Known by their red legs and bills, these dainty gulls nest on isolated headlands and islands.

Over twenty different gull species live in North America. Not all of them live by the ocean, so they should not all be called sea gulls. Ring-billed and California gulls breed far inland and eat insects, a behavior that has earned them the admiration of the Mormons. In 1848, the struggling Mormon colony in Salt Lake City, Utah, faced starvation because the Mormon cricket, a long-horned grasshopper, was destroying all their crops. Large flocks of gulls descended on the plague and saved some of the harvest. Their prayers answered, the Mormons built a monument to the gulls.

Large gulls take four years to get their adult plumage. They start off with muddy-brown feathers and get more gray, white, and black feathers each year until they are adults. Other small gulls, like black-legged kittiwakes and Bonaparte's gulls, change their plumages each year. In the summer, Bonaparte's gulls have black heads. In the winter, they have only a black dot behind the eye.

Gulls are closely related to terns. Since terns cannot glide like gulls, they must always flap their wings.

A California gull devours brine flies.

Terns, sometimes called sea swallows, have long, pointed wings and forked tails. Arctic terns travel over 22,000 miles (35,400 km) each year between the North and South Poles. Terns spend more time in continual sunlight than any other creature on earth. Since the seasons are reversed at the poles, terns enjoy continual daylight in the Arctic, where they summer, and in the Antarctic, where they winter.

Unlike gulls, terns spend little time floating on the water. They fish from the air. Forester's terns hover over their prey and momentarily dip beneath the surface to catch fish in lakes and shallow estuaries. Built like miniature frigatebirds, sooty terns spend up to nine months on the wing. Scientists think these birds can even sleep while flying. Sooty terns are usually unable to land on the water, so they must stay airborne when they pluck food from the surface.

Caspian terns, at just over 1 pound (0.5 kg), are the largest terns in the world. They make quite a splash when they dive from great heights into the water. At 2 ounces (875 g), least terns with their delicate yellow bills are the smallest terns. They are endangered because they nest on beaches frequented by beachgoers.

The Caspian tern can live as long as twenty-five years.

Inca terns nest in rocky crevices.

A colorful South American seabird, the Inca tern has a red mouth, a white mustache, and slate-gray plumage. Fishing in the cold water currents off Peru, this bird is one of two species of terns that nest in cliff holes. The other is the blue-gray noddy, one of the smallest seabirds. The Inca tern flits above the tropical waters picking up marine water striders, the only ocean insect.

In spite of the tern's amazing flying ability, some seabirds are able to take advantage of them. The jaeger, which means hunter in German, is a sea hawk that chases gulls and terns to rob them of their catch. A powerfully built flyer, the jaeger can outmaneuver the fastest seabird. The jaeger can be distinguished from the similar-looking gull by its elongated tail feathers. The parasitic jaeger has sharp, spiked tail feathers. The pomarine jaeger has pom-poms, and the long-tailed jaeger has 10-inch (25-cm) streamers. Another large seabird, the skua, is the largest hunter, acting like a sea eagle when it attacks penguin chicks and other seabirds.

Nesting king penguins stretch nearly as far as the eye can see.

A NEIGHBORHOOD OF NESTS

The sights, sounds, and smells of thousands of nesting seabirds concentrated in one place are unforgettable. A seabird colony is much like a noisy apartment complex where almost every space is filled. Just as seabirds share food resources, they share nesting islands.

By nesting in different areas, many different seabird species can breed on any island. Some types of seabirds, like puffins, nest in deep burrows underground. Others, like auklets, nest in shallow crevices in rocks. Some cormorants nest in trees, while gulls lay eggs on the ground.

Seabirds are usually colored like the sea and rocks where they live. But in the breeding season, colorful beaks, feet, and plumes spice up their gray, black, brown, and white plumage. The seabird species that

Black-browed albatrosses court one another.

develop breeding plumage also change their mates each year. The seabirds that remain in the same plumage all year keep their mates from season to season. The bond between these partners is maintained by courtship dancing and vocalizations at the nest site.

Seabirds do not sing; they mainly squawk and cry. When shearwaters gather together on the breeding grounds at night, they sound like crying babies. Although seabirds may not sound as sweet as song-birds, they sure can dance!

During courtship, seabirds dance in many different ways. Albatrosses dance together, accompanying them-selves with hoots, whinnies, and bill snapping. Blue-footed boobies "strut their stuff" by stepping out with their blue feet. During courtship displays, pigeon guille-mots display their bright-red feet. Sooty terns begin their courtship in the sky. From a swirling mass of fly-ing terns, a pair will rocket out of the flock and streak through the sky almost touching wings. On the ground, they parade around each other with necks out-stretched. The male least tern will even offer a small fish to his prospective mate.

Seabirds lay their eggs according to the amount of available food. When food is abundant and all the

chicks have a chance of surviving, some species will lay several eggs. When food is scarce, seabirds are lucky to raise one chick each year.

Some birds, like the masked booby, have an insurance policy. They lay two eggs. If both eggs hatch, then the firstborn will kill its sibling. If the first egg does not hatch, the second chick will live. Since seabirds are long-lived—albatrosses live up to fifty years—they make up for small family size by reproducing over many years.

Many seabird species nest together on the ground on islands and rocky headlands that border the ocean. Defenseless against many animals, seabirds crowd their nests together in areas that are safe from predators.

When people and their pets do visit seabird colonies, the birds panic and flee. Adult birds stay away as long as people are in the colony. And when parents are not there to shade their young, the hot sun can kill baby birds. Gulls also take advantage of the confusion to raid seabird nests, eating chicks whole and smashing open eggs. It was shipwrecks that first introduced rats, cats, and dogs to many islands. These mammals prey on ground-nesting seabirds. Their populations explode while seabird populations disappear, in some cases never to return.

Albatrosses gather in colonies to nest on mud and grass piles.

OIL AND WATERBIRDS DON'T MIX

Seabirds are sensitive to changes in the weather and in the ocean environment. One such change is a periodic warming of the ocean known as El Niño. El Niño (pronounced el-NEEN-yo) usually occurs around Christmastime in South America and means the child in Spanish. It also occurs elsewhere in the Pacific Ocean any time of year. This warm-water current lowers oxygen levels in the sea surface layers and disrupts the food chain by killing small fish. Seabirds fail to nest, and they may even starve to death. Since severe El Niños occur only once in a while, seabird populations can recover over time.

Man-made changes, however, are longer lasting. For example, in 1989, the *Exxon Valdez* oil spill in

A guillemot, soaked with oil from the
Exxon Valdez tanker spill, rests on oily rocks.

Alaska's Prince William Sound killed many thousands
of seabirds. Oiled birds are unable to keep warm and
risk dying from cold. They also accidentally eat oil
when they preen their feathers, which poisons them.
The oil also poisons the ocean food chain and affects

A group of Adélie penguins head out to sea for food.

fish and other animals for many years. An oil spill not only threatens breeding colonies near the coasts; it may affect the feeding grounds for many miles at sea.

Seabirds also die when they get hooked or tangled in fishing gear. Old plastic fishing nets may float for years at sea, killing many seabirds, as well as fish, porpoises, and seals. Plastic trash dumped into the ocean is also a threat to sea life. Seabirds often mistake small pieces of plastic trash for food. The plastic fills up their stomachs and causes the birds to starve.

Over the years, humans have helped some seabird species. Where fishermen clean their catch at sea, populations of scavengers like the gulls and fulmars have increased greatly. Bridges in the San Francisco Bay provide good nesting places for double-crested cormorants. Where cats and rats have been removed from islands, seabirds have come back to nest. Short-tailed albatrosses have returned from the brink of extinction. Other seabirds, however, still need protection. Just like people, seabirds need clean water and a fresh food supply to survive, where the wind meets the waves.

A NOTE
FROM THE
AUTHOR

Many seabird species, from the yellow-eye penguins to the short-tailed albatrosses, are threatened. To learn about ways to help seabirds, contact Pacific Seabird Group at the following address.

Pacific Seabird Group
Box 179
4505 University Way NE
Seattle, WA 98105

FOR FURTHER READING

Burnie, David. *Bird.* New York: Knopf Books for Young Readers, 1988.

Dewey, Jennifer O. *The Adélie Penguin.* Boston: Little, Brown, 1989.

Gibbons, Gail. *The Puffins Are Back!* New York: HarperCollins, 1991.

Harris, Alan, ed. *Birds.* New York: Dorling Kindersley, 1993.

O'Connor, Karen. *The Herring Gull.* New York: Macmillan, 1992.

Patent, Dorothy H. *Pelicans.* Boston: Houghton Mifflin, 1992.

Sterry, Paul. *Seabirds.* Chatham, N.J.: Raintree Steck-Vaughn, 1994.

Stone, Lynn M. *Penguin.* New York: Macmillan, 1987.

INDEX

Italicized page numbers refer to illustrations.

Jaegers, 49

Kittiwakes, 44
Krill, 11, 41

Labrador ducks, 22

Man o' war birds, 35
Mormon crickets, 44
Murrelets, 21, 22, 24
Murres, 21, 22, *23*

Nests, *8*, 21, *23*, 30,
    51–55, 59
Noddies, 49

Oil spills, 56–59

Pelicans, *11*, 12
Penguins, 13, 15–19, *50*
Plankton, 10–11
Plunge diving, 12
Predators, 16, 19, 55,
    59
Puffins, 13, 21, *26*,
    27, 51

Pursuit diving, 13

Razorbills, *20*
Regurgitation, 30

Seabirds, 9–13, 51–53
    dangers to, 24,
        56–59
    life span of, 55
Shearwaters, 37, 41, 53
Skuas, 49
Squid oil, 37
Storm petrels, 37–38,
    40, 41
Surface seizing, 12

Terns, 12, 35, 44,
    46–49, 53
Totipalmate feet, 29
Tropicbirds, 12, *34*, 35
Tubenoses, 37–41

Underwater flying, 15,
    21

ABOUT
THE AUTHOR

Mark J. Rauzon is an environmental consultant and a writer-photographer who travels widely. He has worked as a biologist for the U.S. Fish and Wildlife Service and served as chair of the Pacific Seabird Group. Mr. Rauzon is the author of several children's books about animals, including *Parrots* for Franklin Watts. He lives in Oakland, California.